GLIMMER

Poems to Find Light in the Darkness

by Shannon Jade

First edition 2026

Text and design by Shannon Jade

ISBN (paperback) 978-1-7641436-3-9

ISBN (ebook) 978-1-7641436-4-6

Published by Wildflower Books

For you,

in hopes that this book

found you when you needed it.

CONTENTS

SHANNON JADE

You start over in the way of *sunlight*.

The delicate colours of dawn

turn the skyline to a tapestry

    of amber and rose,

        lilac and blue.

You are the light through the clouds.

And the morning has come back for you.

— *when the morning returns*

By daybreak,

it isn't so frightening.

The truth of being broken.

These fractured parts

are made for mending,

and light filters *bright*

through the gaps.

— *take your brokenness, and make it art*

There is still good in the world,

if you know how to look for it.

When the darkness threatens

to swallow you whole,

go searching for the light.

— *the darkness will not win*

The night is a heavy truth, a weight

that you don't know how to carry.

But it fractures, falls to pieces all around you.

Something *glitters* bright on the horizon.

And it looks just like *light* in the darkness.

— *glimmering, glittering, true*

Midnight lands like kisses

that taste like starting again.

The day is new,

and you are too,

and all the world

is a great expanse of

POSSIBILITY.

Yours for the taking.

— the power in starting again

The clouds give way

to skies made of colour.

You weather the storm well enough

to find the dazzling light of the rainbow.

— *rainbows wait for you*

Buy yourself flowers.

You deserve them.

Hold someone's hand.

Dance recklessly.

See the world,

and meet new people,

and learn something new every day.

Life is wonderful.

Awe-striking. Wild.

Don't you miss a second of it.

— the wild of the world

Your courage is a miracle of your own making,

not because you face the world unafraid

but because of the way you rise to the challenge,

the way you smile and you laugh when you stumble,

and the way that you promise to try, try again.

— *braver than you believe*

Hope is a verb you have to chase after.

It needs catching like butterflies in nets.

Or the flint that sparks the flame.

The world has not given up you yet,

and it asks only for the same courtesy in return.

Hope is a verb. It needs action.

H O P E is counting on you

to find it fast and make it count.

— *hope is a verb*

On the wings of a butterfly,

life changes its shape again,

and you trust your own wings,

believe they know how to fly.

— *like butterflies*

You are much more than your darkness.

For somebody, you are the *light*.

— *you are the sunbeams*

You are a sunflower,

reaching high,

always turning

towards the light,

following the sun

wherever it roams.

— *sunflower*

Plant seeds deep

in the muddy earth.

Watch the rains turn them

to towering trees,

and follow their lead,

blooming wild

and wondrous

and free.

— *this is how you learn to bloom*

You were not meant

for anything

except

to walk among

the wildflowers

and to whisper

with the wind.

— *walk among wildflowers*

You are music and poetry

and the start of a story.

You are the muse

and the daydream,

made of beauty

and wonder

and love.

— *the story that you are*

You decide to love,

even when it frightens you.

You decide on peace

and hope

and happiness,

so much more powerful

than fear.

— *love is stronger than fear*

Take a moment to watch the sunrise,

rosy gold as it filters through clouds.

Watch for the way of the light

as morning wins out over nightfall.

— *the sunrise wins this round*

Light strikes the surface of the water

and never sinks beneath the waves.

LUMINESCENT.

Shining, gleaming,

floating, flying.

— *the light on the water*

Cerulean coastlines

crash instead of crawling.

Great waves collapse

in a heap at the shore.

And you? You are

the sweeping expanse

of the sprawling seas,

caving in for only a moment

before the current drags you

right back to the place

where you're supposed to be.

— *the current will carry you*

The winter will not last forever.

The ground will thaw,

and the frost will melt.

The summer sun will come home.

— *summer days ahead*

The meaning of life might be laughter.

Might be light in the darkness

or joy in the sadness

or hope in the hard-to-find places.

— *a lesson from nana*

Be so kind and so hopeful

that strangers mistake you for sunshine.

— *be sunshine*

You have been a light in the darkness.

A great force against this heavy tide.

The power of you and impossible things.

My darling, you've finally found sunlight.

— *you find the light*

And the valleys of the earth

give way to the mountains,

reaching for the sky.

— *the mountains rise*

No more storms in teacups.

From the lightest rainfall

to the harshest tempest,

even a hurricane wears itself out

in time enough to make way

for summer sun ...

— *storm in a teacup*

You crash down

like the waves

and rise again

without fear

of striking

the shore.

— *waves crash down*

And I hope
you're proud
of all that
you've become.

— proud of you

For all the battles already won.

— *battles won*

How should I tell you that the worst is finally over?

Your fear falls far behind you and turns to nothing but dust,

the mud and the muck that toughens your skin

so that you are ready for your next adventure.

— *for the future*

You are not just hurting.

You are healing.

— *time to heal*

This pain will not bury you.

You rise taller than the rafters.

— *stronger than the hurt*

What ifs are for more than your worries.

What if you love and don't lose?

What if you learn and you grow?

What if it all works out,

just the way it is supposed to?

— what if, what if, what if...

It is not a burden

to feel everything

this heavy.

It is a gift.

— *the weight of it all*

The world is cruel,

but you are kind,

and that is a powerful thing.

— *kindness over cruelty*

Maybe the world is mapped out for you already,

golden threads leading you

to wherever you're supposed to be.

And so you can't get it wrong

or stray too far from your path.

You're exactly where the universe needs you.

— *the threads of fate*

There will never be

a perfect time

to chase your dreams,

so start now.

Give up

on holding yourself back

from building a life

made of starlight.

— *begin today*

The fire calls you home, and you let it.

Ignite me, you whisper.

Embers spark, and smoke billows.

Flames climb higher all around you.

You never feel them burn.

You crumble to the ashes

and call yourself a wasteland

in the moments before your wings unfurl again,

rise stronger from cinders and dust.

— *the phoenix rising*

Look up to the sky,

and find stories in the stars,

CONSTELLATIONS

glittering bright

in the shapes of courage and wishes and miracles.

— the stars align for you

We shimmer and sparkle

and catch at the light

and do not give

to cobwebs or rust.

The world is shining

like dew drops,

like diamonds

and crystals

and stars.

— *things that shine*

Reach the skies,

and run your fingers

through the clouds.

Let raindrops

sting your skin

in the shapes

of dreams that matter.

— *dreams like dew drops*

When the storm strikes, it is easy to listen for thunder,

  roaring like something that hungers.

Or to feel the wind lashing,

rain stinging your skin.

Or to find heavy stormclouds, gun-metal grey,

rolling high over the hills.

Lightning flashes for only moment

before it disappears from the sky

and leaves no trace behind.

But for just an instant,

      a flicker,

            a spark,

the winter dark lifted,

made way for something with power,

cleared space for a sharp burst of *light*.

— *lightning in the storm*

Drink tea, and eat cake, and sing badly,

and wake up in time to watch the sunrise,

and love with reckless abandon,

brave and honest and free.

There is so much magic in this world,

and I promise it's yours if you want it.

— *the magic you deserve*

The world you wish for has a different shape

from the harsh-angled world you know.

It is softer at the edges and strong enough

to withstand the floods, the fires, the storms.

It is a dream, and you don't quite trust it,

a glamour that flickers when you look too closely.

But you don't give in on believing

in the power of a brighter tomorrow.

And that's at least half of the fight.

— *a world worth believing in*

You are a wildflower,

and you were made

to weather the storm.

— *with the strength of wildflowers*

In this racing world,

you stop to find

just a moment of peace.

— *quiet and calm*

The world is turning.

The sun is shining.

It's going to be okay.

Promise.

— *it all works out in the end*

Just when you think the light is a fallacy,

the first sunbeams climb to the horizon,

and you recognise the dawn once again.

— *when night fades to morning*

Then the light is more

than myth and legend.

It is a promise you believe in.

That the brightest days are not far behind you.

That the future is made of sunbeams and fireflies.

And dreams that really do come true.

— *the promise of tomorrow*

Then you remember that joy is not a faraway fallacy,

not a make-believe dream or an empty promise.

Instead, it is a choice.

You decide to be happy.

You find joy in the tiny moments.

You plant it like seeds and watch it grow.

— *happiness you choose*

Someday soon, the dark will turn to light,

and this will all be a story of how you survived.

— oh, what a story it will be

There is light in this heavy darkness.

There is love with more power than hatred.

There is hope, when it's hardest to find.

— *light and love and hope, even now*

When you're making mistakes,

you're really making memories.

Do not fear the weight of failing.

The best stories are rough at the edges.

— *the memories you make*

You do not choose whether you fail.

You choose whether you fight.

— *it's no easy thing to stumble*

Consider these

not as setbacks

but stepping stones,

the path that leads the way.

— *step boldly forward*

When the world locked down and went quiet,

or when it sounded much too booming loud.

Song notes fill the heavy air with joy again,

a balm for grief and sorrow and loneliness.

So when there is nothing else for it, let there be music.

Listen for voices singing songs of hope,

just when you thought we'd all lost it.

— *still, we keep singing*

It's a gift to care so deeply

that you feel it like an ache in your chest.

To wish and dream and hope and love

so fiercely that it finds no place else to land.

— your empathy is not your weakness

You could not plan for the darkness.

But my goodness.

Someday, you will find it.

All this glittering,

shimmering

LIGHT.

— *to who you used to be*

The rains collapse to dusty soils

and turn mudbanks to fields of green.

Your tears are not your weakness

but your strength for trying again.

— *tears like rain*

You need not fear the thundering rains.

Remember that you are the storm,

the hurricane,

spiralling wild,

the power of the wind

and the tempest.

— *as strong as the storm*

I hope you believe

in the wonder you are,

that you never underestimate

your own magic.

— *my hope for you*

And if the soils

where you are planted

will not let you grow,

then perhaps

it is time

to kick up your roots

and search

for greener pastures...

— *the places where you bloom*

Wish on stars and on dandelions

and on feathers in the wind,

and believe the best wishes come true.

— *all the best wishes*

Count your love
and all your luck.
Find the beauty
In the ugliness.

— *isn't it lovely*

Grateful for all these second chances.

— *you can try again*

If every cloud

has a silver lining,

then these skies

must be made of gold.

— *clouds lined with gold*

Your dreams rest light in the palm of your hands

and offer chances at turning to truth.

So do not let your wishes wither.

Send them to the stars, and teach them to fly

on wings that know nothing of gravity.

— *sometimes, dreams do come true*

Sometimes,

it is so much more

than enough

just to wait

for the spring

and to trust

that there

will be

flowers.

— *the spring is on its way*

How hopeful

to believe

that

in every day

there is

a chance

to start again.

— tomorrow is another chance

You are the

SMOKECLOUDS,

climbing high in the sky.

You are the

EMBERS,

rising from the

ASHES.

— *in the wake of the fire*

Call yourself lightning,

and sing like the thunder.

Dance under storm clouds,

and kiss in the rain.

Love like you're not scared of falling.

Run and jump and skip and try,

and hope against odds, with all of your might.

— *be the storm*

The great shadows of greater trees

tower high above the earth.

Reaching skywards, catching clouds.

You don't pause to question

the weight of gravity.

Instead, you find footholds

in the mud and the bark,

climb as far as the old branches will take you.

— the trees that tower high

If you cannot find sunlight,

find moonbeams.

Know the shape

of the night's brightest light.

— *the sun and the moon*

What a wonderful day,

dawning with fresh possibilities.

— the promise of every new morning

You grow like the tallest of trees,

reach higher towards the clouds

and snatch at starbeams,

catch moonlight in the palm of your hand.

— *you are the forest, reaching*

The hard days need not harden you.

— *proud to be gentle*

You will laugh until your stomach hurts

and sing yourself hoarse in the wind.

You will streak your skin in mud

and smell flowers by the roadside.

You will find music like magic

and fall in love with strangers.

There are so many bright days ahead.

— *great joy waits for you*

Blue but not with melancholy.

Blue like the great expanse

of sweeping summertime skies.

— *a better blue*

The earth trembles beneath you,

and you do not trust the shape of it.

It threatens to send you tumbling.

But you won't let it.

You stumble, but you stand your ground.

It's time now for trying again.

— *you do not fall; you fly*

Look for the colours of flowers,

blooming through the mudbanks.

Grow violet and cobalt,

honey and rose,

brighter for the weight of the dirt.

— *claim your colours, bright*

The helpers and heroes

climb up from the rubble,

with the weight of bright hope

on their shoulders.

— *look for the helpers and heroes*

When the silence

weighs too heavy,

listen for music.

And if you cannot hear it,

lift your voice and sing.

— *make your own music*

Trust in tomorrow.

You are right on time.

— *you are not falling behind*

All that you lose

is experience you gain,

so don't be too scared

to take chances.

— *the things you win*

You deserve a beautiful life,

the kind you don't ever have to run away from.

— *this life of yours*

Oh, it's all so beautiful.

This world made of wonder and wishes.

— *the world is made of wonder*

See the world through
rose-coloured glasses,
the blush of the sun
as it rises in the morning.

— *rosy, bright*

In anger, offer kindness.

In fear, turn to hope.

In darkness, share the light.

— *contrast is everything*

You believe there is magic left in this world,

and if you can't find it, you'll build it with kindness.

— *to be kind is its own magic*

When war wages,

find the power of peacetime.

Forge hope as an act of rebellion.

— *rebel in hope*

All the stardust has already fallen,

and all the earth is made of wishes.

— *wishes upon the brightest stars*

You are someone in love again,

with a person, with a place, or with you.

— *all that you love*

Be proud of the person you're becoming
and the battles it took to find them.

— *who you are now*

You don't know anything at all

except that every time

you thought the world was ending,

the very shape of it collapsing

all around you,

the night faded

to the dim light of dawn,

and the sun climbed

over the horizon,

and the flowers bloomed

in the dewy grasses,

and nature will out,

it went on.

— *sure enough, life carries on*

You look beyond the shadows
and find that they only appear
in the wake of the light.

— *the shadow's inception*

Believe me there is beauty

in all these broken pieces.

— *just like kintsugi*

So love the things you love fiercely.

Hold tight to the things

that bring you joy.

— *guard your happiness*

Kiss strangers.

Give compliments.

Watch the sunset.

Swim in the ocean.

Live bold and bright

and with love and light.

Treat the world as the miracle it is.

— *the miracle of it all*

A daisy reaches skyward from my humble window sill.

A hiker sees the sunrise from a sweeping, rolling hill.

You hear soft voices singing as the stars puncture the sky.

A forest thickens with the weight of trees that tower high.

The days are sometimes harsh.

The nights are cold when they arrive.

But kindness waits for finders. How kind just to be alive.

— *kindness waits for finders*

Give your love freely.

Lend your light to the world.

— *your light and love*

Fireflies like fairy lights.

Magic is not such a mystery.

It is light dancing across the dark sky.

— find the fairy lights

The flowers climb up through the mud banks,

and the sun rises gold in the morning.

The waves crash heavy to the shore,

peaks of the water shining like diamonds.

And you can find pictures in the clouds,

coloured rosy pink, halfway to thunder and lightning.

The forests breathe slowly, in the shapes of swaying trees.

Shadows roam over barren lands,

proof that any place can be a home if you let it.

Somewhere, the desert air shimmers,

hazy and glittering in the weight of the heat,

a mirage playing tricks at dreaming.

All this wide world, built of wonder and power.

And you say you don't believe in magic?

— *magic is all around us*

ACKNOWLEDGEMENTS

This world has plenty of darkness, but I believe that poetry can shed just a little bit of *light*.

I'd like to say thank you to my mum, who is my first reader and my greatest supporter. To friends and family who continue to support my creative journey. To the wonderful reading and poetry communities who inspire me and encourage me to be a better writer every day.

I'd like to acknowledge the traditional custodians of the beautiful lands where I live, write, and dream.

Last but certainly not least, I want to thank *you*. If you have read this book and gained even a morsel of hope from one of the poems in it, thank you. Thank you for reading, hoping, trying again, and remembering to look for the glimmers.

ABOUT THE AUTHOR

Shannon Jade is an author and environmental scientist who believes in the real-world magic of storytelling. She is the author of *A Song for the Earth*, which earned bronze prize for book of the year at the 2025 ABLE Golden Book Awards and became an IngramSpark nature poetry bestseller, stocked at over 100 bookstores internationally. Today, Shannon writes poetry with a hopeful environmental focus, aiming to make the world a better, greener, and kinder place. For acting, modelling, singing, and media opportunities, Shannon is represented by Stacey at ZBD Talent.

www.ingramcontent.com/pod-product-compliance
Lightning Source LLC
Chambersburg PA
CBHW011739020426
42333CB00024B/2961